Olympic Champion Wilma Rudolph

Grace Castle

ROSEN COMMON CORE READERS

Rosen Classroom™

New York

Published in 2014 by The Rosen Publishing Group, Inc.
29 East 21st Street, New York, NY 10010

Book Design: Mickey Harmon

Photo Credits: Cover, p. 5 Jerry Cooke/Contributor/Sports Illustrated/Getty Images; pp. 7 (background), 11, 19 ASSOCIATED PRESS/AP Images.com; p. 7 (map) Lightspring/Shutterstock.com; p. 9 PhotoQuest/Contributor/Archive Photos/Getty Images; p. 13 Mondadori/Contributor/Mondadori/Getty Images; p. 15 Boris Sosnovyy/Shutterstock.com; p. 17 James Whitmore/Contributor/Time & Life Pictures/Getty Images; p. 21 Tomtom at Hebrew Wikipedia/Wikipedia.org; p. 22 sunsetman/Shutterstock.com.

ISBN: 978-1-4777-2385-2
6-pack ISBN: 978-1-4777-2386-9

Manufactured in the United States of America

CPSIA Compliance Information: Batch #CS13RC: For further information contact Rosen Publishing, New York, New York at 1-800-237-9932.

Contents

Famous Athlete

Wilma Rudolph is an important person in American sports history. She was a famous track star in the 1960s. People called her the fastest woman in the world.

Although she won several races at the **Olympics** and became a **champion**, Wilma's life wasn't easy. She grew up sick, poor, and at a time when African Americans didn't have equal rights.

Wilma Rudolph had a hard childhood, but it made her a stronger person.

AAU
USA

A Star Is Born

Wilma's life is an interesting story. She was born in St. Bethlehem, Tennessee, on June 23, 1940. Her family was really big. She had 21 brothers and sisters!

The other Rudolph children always played sports. Wilma wanted to play sports just like them. However, nobody ever thought she would be able to. That's because she was very sick as a child.

Wilma was the third youngest of all her brothers and sisters.

Wilma Rudolph
St. Bethlehem
Tennessee

Wilma was born prematurely (pree-muh-CHUR-lee). That means she was born earlier than she was supposed to be. She weighed only 4.5 pounds (2 kg) when she was born. Many doctors thought she wouldn't live long.

Because Wilma was born prematurely, her body was weak. When she was 4, she got sick from a virus called polio.

Polio isn't a problem anymore. In the 1950s, Dr. Jonas Salk created a way to keep people from getting polio.

Polio is a virus that affected many children in the 1940s and 1950s. The polio virus caused Wilma to lose the use of her left leg. Her doctors said that she might not walk ever again.

Wilma wore a metal brace on her leg for 5 years. She also had to wear special shoes. At home, her family rubbed her legs to try and help her get better.

Today, doctors know how to keep kids from getting polio.

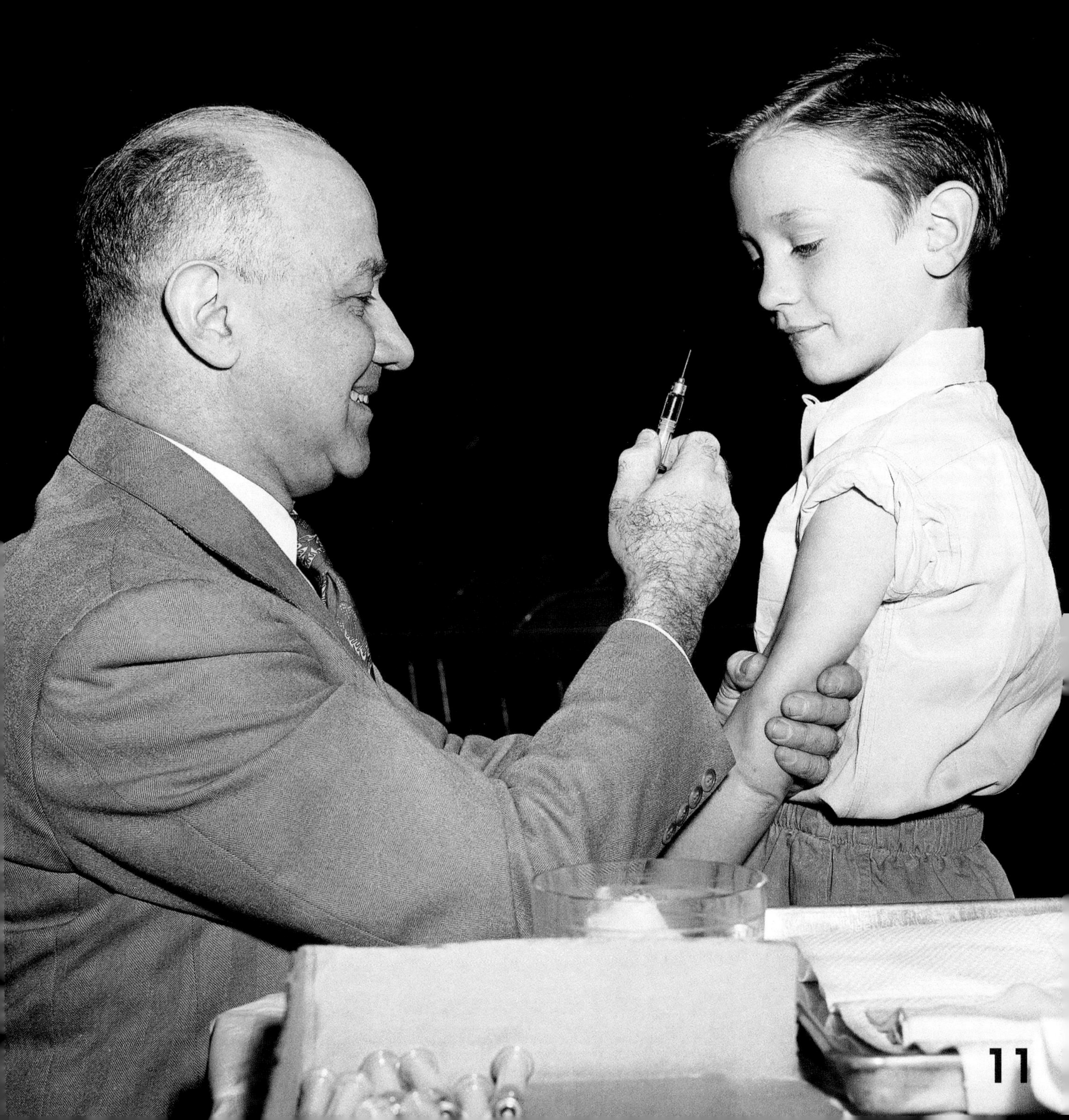

Meeting Coach Temple

Nobody ever thought Wilma would be good at sports, but she worked hard to become a talented **athlete**. She joined her high school's basketball team. Playing basketball brought her a lot of joy.

Then, when Wilma was 14, she met a track **coach** named Ed Temple. He knew he could teach her how to be a good runner. It changed her life forever.

Ed Temple was a track coach at Tennessee State University.

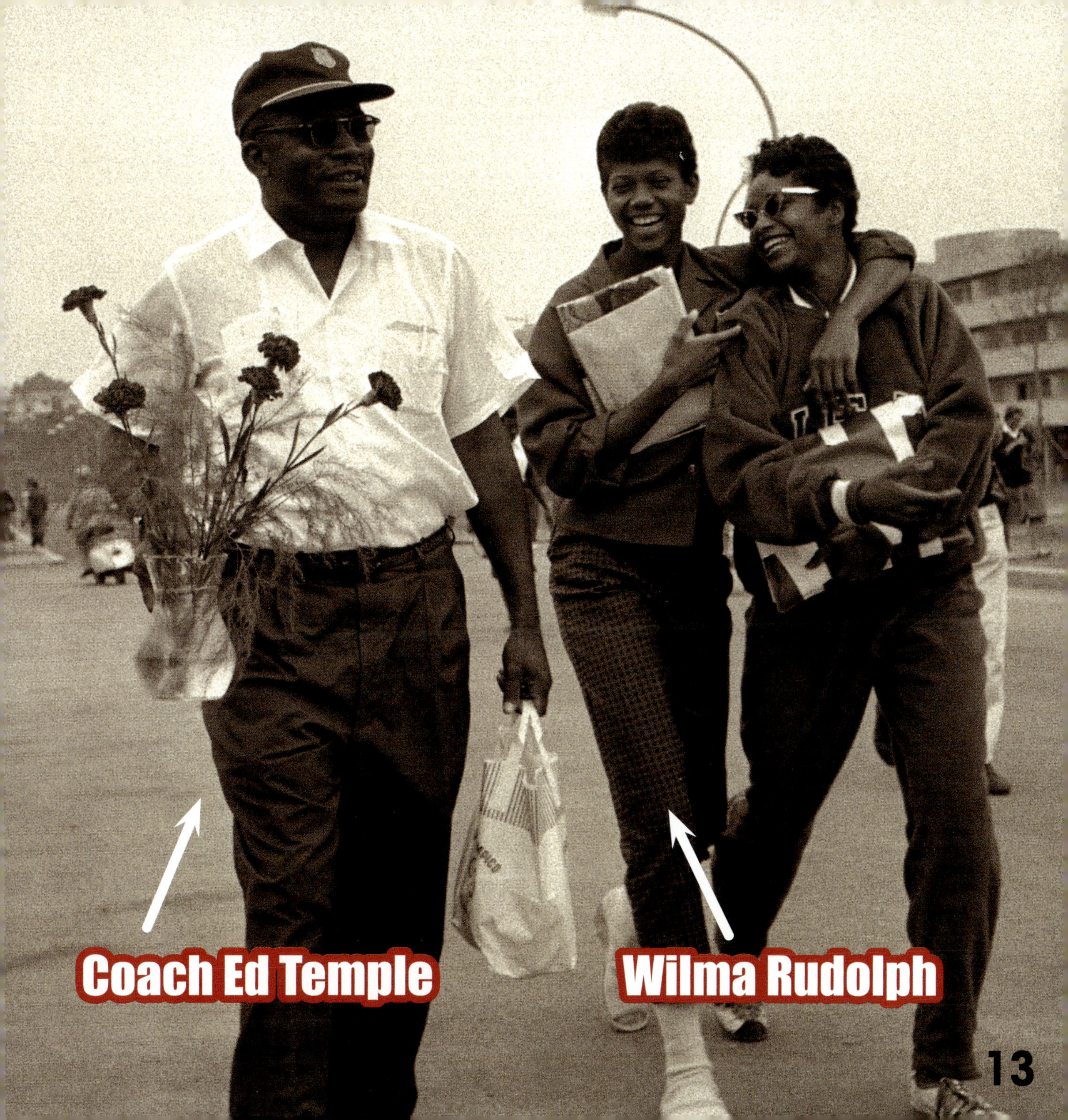
Coach Ed Temple
Wilma Rudolph

Ed Temple worked at a college in Wilma's town. He helped her join a summer track team at the college. Wilma knew he would be a good teacher.

By the time Wilma was 16, she was fast enough to go to the 1956 Summer Olympics in Melbourne, Australia. She and her team won a bronze medal in a track event called the 4x100 relay.

A medal is a piece of metal that you get when you win something. Bronze medals are given to athletes who come in third place.

2
1

Back to the Olympics

Wilma finished high school and went to college at Tennessee State University. She continued to run for the track team. She knew she could get to the Olympics again.

At only 20 years old, Wilma went to the 1960 Summer Olympics in Rome, Italy, prepared to take home the gold medal. The whole world was watching to see how well she would race.

It was very hot during the 1960 Summer Olympics. Some people worried this would make it hard to run.

People couldn't believe how fast Wilma was. She ran the 100-meter dash in 11 seconds flat! Her next event was the 200-meter dash. She ran it in 23.5 seconds.

Wilma's last event was a 400-meter relay race. She and her teammates ran it in 44.5 seconds. Wilma became the first American woman to win three gold medals in track and field in a single Olympics.

Wilma won gold medals in all her events at the 1960 Summer Olympics.

The Gazelle

People all over the world loved Wilma for being an Olympic champion. People said she was the fastest woman in history. In France, they called her the "gazelle."

Wilma died in 1994. Many people cried when they heard the news. Today, we remember her as one of the fastest people who ever lived!

Wilma won the Associated Press Athlete of the Year Award in 1960, and again in 1961.

Wilma's Life

1940	Wilma is born.
1944	Wilma gets sick from polio, losing the use of her left leg.
1949	Wilma gets her leg brace off.
1954	Ed Temple discovers Wilma at a basketball game.
1956	Wilma wins a bronze medal at her first Olympic Games.
1960	Wilma wins three gold medals at the Olympics.
1962	Wilma retires from running.
1994	Wilma dies.

Glossary

athlete (ATH-leet) A person who has trained to be very good at a sport.

champion (CHAM-pee-uhn) Somebody who is the best at something.

coach (KOHCH) A person who trains or teaches others.

Olympics (uh-LIHM-pihks) A series of international sporting events held once every two years.

Index